POSITIVE
THINKING
ACTION

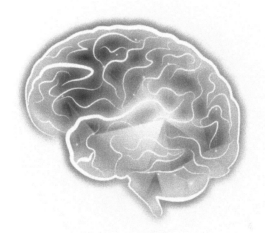

7 POWERFUL
SECRETS
POSITIVE
THINKING

INDEX

POSITIVE THINKING ACTION

Introduction

Chapter 1: Being around positive people

Chapter 2: Using Positive Affirmations

Chapter 3: Avoiding Negative Thinking

Chapter 4: Setting Goals

Chapter 5: Thanks

Chapter 6: Surround yourself with the positive

Chapter 7: Getting organized

Chapter 8: Stay Focused

Chapter 9: Using Time Wisely

Chapter 10: Getting the Right Attitude

Conclusion

7 POWERFUL SECRETS POSITIVE THINKING

Introduction

First secret: The Mind/Body Connection

Second secret: Emotions and their effect on well-being

Third secret: How to control your thinking

Fourth secret: How to react to external events in your life

Fifth secret: Enjoy a productive life... with positive thoughts

Sixth secret: Looking for the good

Seventh secret: It's not always easy

POSITIVE
THINKING
ACTION

BOOK 1

POSITIVE THINKING ACTION

Introduction

When we put on the news today there's hardly any good news.

Moving stories seem few and far between. It is difficult to be positive with so many negative facts that influence each and every one of us today.

To become positive in our thinking we need to focus on things that inspire and uplift us. If we can alter our point of view and eliminate the negative thoughts that invade our minds they will make us happier.

If you find it difficult to defeat a negative attitude, then this book can benefit you by giving you some positive attitude tips that you can apply in your daily life. That's easier said than done, isn't it? Why not...Try it...

Here are the ten steps to success through positive thinking many people have benefited from using these tips to stop negative thinking and build a more positive attitude.

Chapter 1: Being around positive people

Surround yourself with successful and positive people. It is amazing how the influence of other people can impact and touch our own personal energy. Positive individuals energize us and drive us to grow in our belief that we can achieve what we set out to do. Get rid of negative people who ultimately dismantle any progress you make.

The Right People

Positive people seem to have an energy supply that never seems to let them down, and they achieve the great goals in life that they desire and dream of. They can help you stay on track and give you energy to achieve your own goals. Many times these successful individuals share the same goals you have and are often very generous in passing on their wisdom and strategies.

So how do you discover these positive, like-minded people?

Here are some tips to help you find them, network with them, and get useful information and advice:

Smile

Although it may seem ridiculous, smiling can

immediately attract people to you - particularly other positive individuals. Having and showing a good perspective on life's ups and downs makes others want to be around you. It's often difficult to be positive day in and day out, so people often look for a way to be more optimistic. If you are a friendly and welcoming person, and show the world with your smile, people will see you as an optimistic person.

You've probably heard that it takes less muscle to smile than to frown, so not only will you be conveying positivity to the world, but you'll also be saving energy.

Transmitting positively

Although we all have difficult days when

nothing seems to be going right, the last thing you want to do is talk and complain incessantly. Nobody likes a belly button, right?

For example, if someone were to ask you, "How are you today? Don't answer negatively. Instead, take a minute - and a breath - and then respond with optimism, even if you're having a difficult day. After all, positive people don't waste their time or energy on negative individuals.

It can be really hard to feel positive in the face of life's challenges, and I don't advise you to suppress your emotions. So either you clean up the things that are hard to deal with or you choose to focus on what's working.

Even if you don't feel so positive, if you stay optimistic in your outlook, you will attract positive people to you.

Think Positively

Thinking positively even through disappointments will help you see the good in every state of affairs and attract positive people who share this vision.

Even if you don't really subscribe to these positive thoughts at first, or you find that positive thinking is difficult, engaging in negative talk about yourself will help you think positively and produce new positive thought patterns in your brain. Over time, positive thinking will become easier and more innate.

We all have energy within us and we have the choice to use it in a constructive or destructive way. Pay attention to the positive people in your life and you will notice that they try to be cheerful and optimistic, even in difficult times.

Behave positively

It is not appropriate to smile, communicate and think positively when pursuing a goal. You must also take action!

For example, maybe you thought you could get a promotion in the past, but then you just sat back and did nothing while someone else did. This time your new positive thinking

14

will have transformed you into a positive person who takes positive action!

Showing your boss and colleagues that you are proactive and positive will prepare you for more success.

Extend

Finally, reach out to people in your work, in your circle of friends, or even to people on the street who seem to live positively. Ask them what helps them stay positive and achieve their goals.

Finding positive people will give you useful information to help you reach your goals and help you succeed; it will help you establish a network of positive friends and role models.

Being positive and exemplifying positivity attracts other people.

After all, what is equal attracts what is equal.

People enjoy being around others with similar attitudes, and by maintaining a positive outlook, you're sure to lead yourself to the successful people you seek.

Chapter 2: Using Positive Affirmations

Think of a positive statement and repeat it often.

Positive affirmations can create surprising results in your thinking process. For example, if you write that you are always depressed, and then your affirmation might be, "I am happy to be in control. Repeat your affirmations many times a day and feel the power of positive thinking.

Creating Affirmations

All Positive Statements are not created equal; in fact some may even be detrimental to changing the habit, paradigm or mood you are trying to change. For example, if you are trying to quit smoking, but you use the statement - I won't - by having - "no" ‖ in your statement you may be reinforcing your smoking habit since the mind tends to omit the "no".

Also, the affirmation is in future tense by having the word in it, so your subconscious interprets that it is not something you want to do right now, but that you are waiting.

Positive affirmations should be expressed in the present tense.

-Right now (present tense) should be used instead of -I'll do- (future tense).

Positive affirmations can be stated in the first or second person.

Research has shown that some individuals respond better to first-person statements, but others may react better to second-person statements personal‖ (you). I would suggest using both... why not cover all the bases

Positive Statements should be specific.

Research in recent years has shown that the more specific the statement, the more likely it is that the desired result will be achieved. -I'm happy and grateful to be at my ideal weight of 115 kilos is better than -I'm happy and grateful to be at my ideal weight. However, I have no doubt that even the non-specific affirmation would give you a better sense of overall well-being if used consistently.

Positive Affirmations call for repetition to produce results.

When it comes to affirmations, repetition is king. For the subconscious to act you need to hear or see the affirmation repeatedly. Can you imagine what would happen if the subconscious only needed a couple of repetitions to act? Our lives would be in chaos.

Positive Affirmations are best used with emotion.

Simple robotic repetition of an affirmation will not create the same results as an affirmation that is mixed with emotion.

Since we are all a little different, it might be helpful to look at some of the different emotions you have and see how you can incorporate them into your affirmation.

Positive statements should not produce any negative side effects.

Be careful in producing affirmations that you only get the results you want. Using an affirmation such as - I am determined to lose weight and will do whatever it takes to achieve my goal - may result in your subconscious saying - okay, I can handle that command - that it should help you lose some real weight.

Positive Affirmations should be realistic.

It's great to use affirmations to help us swallow even our biggest challenges, but our affirmations, like our goals, should be based on reality (even though the truth is often what we think it is). For example, if you've

always had a mentality of poverty but use a claim that you're richer than Bill Gates, I predict that you'll spend a lot of time waiting for that claim to become evident.

Positive Claims should be short and sweet.

Affirmations should be long enough to be particular but not so long that they cannot be easily restated or remembered.

Positive Affirmations should be used consistently.

Using an affirmation from time to time when you think about it will probably only make you think the affirmations don't work; they need to be used consistently. Your

subconscious helps you to fulfill your heart's true desires and would probably not interpret an occasional affirmation as a true desire. I recommend at least 30 days of the same affirmation, or more if necessary.

Positive Affirmations are best used in conjunction with visualization.

The more ways you can impress your subconscious with your desires, the greater the chances of success. Writing your affirmation on a card that you can carry with you and reading it at any time will help your affirmation manifest even more. For some affirmations you can use a photo as a visual affirmation, such as an old photo when you were at the weight you want to be now, or possibly your head stuck on someone else's body.

Positive Affirmations need execution to work.

The affirmation without execution will probably not manifest. Positive Affirmations, which are a very powerful tool, are not like your own personal genius - most of the things you'd like to change will require some action, like telling yourself to stop when you're about to do something that isn't in coalition with what you say your goal is. Even the easy action of reading your affirmation card at every opportunity can produce surprising results.

Positive Affirmations work best when used with a feeling of gratitude.

Saying an affirmation with a sense of gratitude does a few things; first, it opens your heart to receive it - if you don't have a sense of gratitude you're not in a receptive state of mind, and second, it is affirming that you already possess what you are affirming - which becomes true as soon as you accept it.

Chapter 3: Avoiding Negative Thinking

When you start using positive affirmations in your daily life, avoiding negative thinking is just as crucial. Even though this is easier said than done, it is a must. It will take patience and perseverance, but you can remove the negative by thinking. Your success depends on blocking negative thoughts.

Eliminating Bad Thoughts

Stopping being negative is like stopping any other bad habit - the more serious the bad habit, the harder it is to move on the opposite side. Just as it is easier for someone who smokes two cigarettes a day to quit than for someone who smokes two packs a day, someone who has an occasional negative thought will feel more comfortable than someone who is a chronic belly button. But don't worry if you are in the last class, as long as your commitment is firm, you will be able to transform your life.

Here are some tips to help you eliminate negative thoughts from your life:

Set a realistic goal to reduce your negativity

Saying that you will never have another negative thought is unrealistic and will only make you fail. In most examples, it won't happen overnight, so anticipate that the

whole process will take about a month.

Surround yourself with individuals who are positive

You don't have to get rid of your friends who are negative, but try to excuse yourself when the conversation turns negative and you don't participate in pity parties. ||

Be aware of when you allow negativity to affect you and stop it. Turn it into something positive by thinking to yourself - I found myself saying something negative so I wouldn't do it again next time.||

Reward yourself when you avoid being negative.

Again, keep in mind that your goal here is to reduce the amount of negativity in your life and not to eliminate it completely (if you can do the latter, more power to you). Ironically, popular media portrays positive people in a negative way: naive, strange, out of touch, annoying, unpleasant, and unpleasant. This is because when individuals are happy and satisfied they have no need to avoid reality by overeating, drinking alcohol, taking drugs (both narcotics and prescription) and burying themselves in television, movies and celebrity gossip to forget about their atrocious lives.

It's perfectly absurd to think this way since in reality positive people are just the opposite:

popular, successful and happy. Here's an extra tip that will help you eliminate the negativity: turn off the TV and spend some quality time with the people you love.

Chapter 4: Setting Goals

This is a really crucial step that will help you succeed in changing your negativity into a more positive mindset. When you set realistic goals that will help you stay focused.

Achieving an attainable goal will increase your positive outlook.

If you set a goal to earn a million dollars in a month that most likely won't happen, it will only destroy the efforts you've made...to be more positive.

Look Ahead

These basic tips are organized in a sequence that will help you move from thinking about your goals to actually achieving them. These are just suggestions, take what you like and try it out for a while to see what works best for you.

1. Use a journal to keep track of your journey towards your goals where you can keep daily or weekly records of your progress, including affirmations, successes, appreciation for your hard work, reinforcements, resistances, obstacles, etc. Use your goal journal to write down your goals initially and to rewrite them over time. Use it to break down your goals into steps. Review your progress regularly and take some notes.

2. Put yourself in a positive state before you write down your goals: It is really crucial to put yourself in an inspired, positive and relaxed state before you write down your goals. Some ideas for getting into a positive state include Meditation, listening to inspirational music, reading something fun or entertaining, watching a funny movie, taking a walk in a naturally beautiful place, exercising quickly, reading or listening to an inspirational story, listening to motivational tapes, exercising quickly or praying.

3. Start brainstorming: After getting into a good mental and emotional state, the brainstorming begins. Write down all potential goals quickly without editing or criticizing. You can review and prioritize later; right now you want to be as creative

and great at your vision as you are able to be.

4. Areas of your life that you should consider in setting your goals: Here are a number of potential areas of your life to consider when formulating your goal list: Career, finances, relationships, family, home, friends, personal development, well-being, appearance, possessions, fun and recreation, travel, spiritual, self-esteem and service/community.

Some types of goals include: personal development such as emotional, mental, physical and spiritual.

5. Timeframe of Goals: Goals are found in different time periods such as: Immediate goals, 30 day goals, 6 month goals, 1 year

goals, 5 years, 10 years or more. Make sure you are able to achieve what you want within the time frame.

6. Here are 4 tips for writing effective goal statements: Say it like it already happened: When you write your goal, say it like it already happened. Put your goals in words that assume you have already achieved them. For example, -Now I have a new 2002 silver 4-door BMW sedan.‖

Use motivating language: To make you passionate, engaged and motivating, add emotional language to your written goals. Here's an example - I love and am excited about my beautiful new house in the hills-‖ which is much more exciting than - I like my new house in the hills-‖.

Writing specifically and in detail - As your subconscious manifests things literally, you want to write particular and detailed goals. Use language that is clear in describing exactly what you want in positive rather than negative terms: Examples of positive statements might be -Now I'm free from the habit of fumar||, or -Now I'm a smoke-free individual||. Examples of negative statements might be -I don't smoke at dias|| or -I'm not a smoker-||.

7. Make sure these are really your goals: Check with yourself to make sure you are thinking about what you really want. We often try to please others at our expense. You will not succeed in achieving the goals your parents, spouse, or other friends or relatives want for you.

8. Be Consistent in Goal Setting: Consider your most crucial values and beliefs in setting your goals (e.g., honesty, safety, integrity, freedom, responsibility, respect for others, love, leadership, etc.). For example, if you value freedom, your goal may be to be self-employed.

If you value safety, you may want to work for the government, where layoffs rarely occur.

9. Choose rational goals: select goals that you can actually achieve in a reasonable time frame. An example of a rational goal might be:

-I am 55 years old and want to sing opera with a local light opera performance group, a choir, or monthly recitals with my voice teacher's students‖ (given, of course, that you have a good voice). An irrational goal might be: -I'm 55, I've never taken singing lessons, and I want to be a world-class opera singer playing key roles with the New York Metropolitan Opera‖. It is unlikely that someone starting at 55 can do this, even with an excellent voice and rigorous training.

10. Prioritize your goals: After brainstorming, one way to prioritize is to put the highest priority goals on ten of the ten possible points and the lowest on one of the ten.

Choose 3 to 7 of the goals with high numbers and focus your efforts only on them for the next few months. Try not to choose too many goals to focus on, as this will dilute your energy and make it harder to get the results you want.

11. Create a step-by-step plan: Divide each goal into manageable blocks by creating a step-by-step plan for achieving it. For example, if you want a new car, first decide exactly what color, model, year and brand you want. Write this down in your goal journal.

Then write down the particular steps you need to take to reach your goal such as: applying for a car loan, looking at and trying out different models, writing statements, visualizing yourself driving the car, and so on.

Chapter 5: Thanks

When you appreciate all the positive things in your life, no matter how small, it will help you succeed and extinguish the negativity. Focusing on these good things will make the challenges you face significantly less important and more easily addressed.

Say thank you

When something bad happens, instead of accepting it and taking it personally, we need to learn to change the way we think about it. For example, if you work in the service industry and you have a rude client, instead of letting him ruin your day and your mood, try to show some compassion, maybe something bad has happened to that individual, try to do something good for him. A smile can be contagious. Instead of taking everyone's bad moods personally, choose to be in a good mood, smile, and spread joy.

With life's big problems that can bring us down, like a sick family member, a divorce, a disagreement with a loved one, throw away your worries. Do what you can to help or correct the situation and then leave it in God's hands.

You are only one person, you cannot fix everything and you should not have to carry the whole burden of life in your heart day after day. Do your best to apologize to those who have hurt you, forgive those who have hurt you, ask for help when you need it and offer help when you can.

It's about letting go of all those things that are in your heart that keep you from having a positive outlook. It's your choice, you are able to keep the negative or let it go to make room for the positive.

Some people will never tell you they had a bad day. In fact, some believe there is no such thing as a bad day. This was a difficult concept for me to understand... for me, "bad days" had been a constant occurrence. For some, every day is a gift.

Some are grateful for challenges as they are taught, they are grateful for their work even when it is not pleasant. They adopt skills to see each day as a "good day" no matter what has happened. When I started trying to adopt this philosophy I detected that it worked! Just when I decided in my mind that I was having a "bad day" I would try to discover something good in it, when I discovered something good I realized that a few bad things don't ruin a whole day unless you stop! It's a choice!

Every day we are alive is a gift for which there is much to be thankful, so why do we focus on the things that make us unhappy?

Readjust your thinking... Bad days are choices we make!

In the end, having a positive outlook is up to you! It's a choice we make every day. You can never control what others say or do to you, but you can control your response. By choosing the positive path, as briefly outlined above, you will be happier and healthier than ever before. You will have a peace within you that will leave people looking at you in wonder. I think this is a choice worth making.

Chapter 6: Surround yourself with the positive

For me, listening to motivational material is empowering and stimulating, but at the same time relaxing and reassuring.

Take advantage of the wealth of data on personal achievement that is available today, you, too, will soon be hooked on success.

Over the past fifty years or so, incredible progress has been made in the areas of achievement and personal development. Individuals have committed their entire lives to the study of success. Their life's work has been summarized in the books and audio platforms they have launched. Many of these books and platforms are like hidden gems on bookstore shelves and in storage, waiting for readers to find the life-changing information stored inside.

If these books and plans are really so powerful, why don't many people read and listen to them? Here are the basic causes:

- They don't think the data will help them. This is the most difficult obstruction for successful writers to overcome. It takes belief, or faith, for a person to start reading a book, start listening to a course of audio study, or start a program like this. Ironically, many of these plans contain information that will help establish the necessary faith; however, those who do not have at least a little confidence, or the will to keep an open mind, will never take that step.

- The self-help content has become a disgusting "rap". In some cases, this is well deserved. There are a few writers, particularly on the subject of income, who are, well... let's just say less than certified to give advice. If you buy a book on how to make a million dollars, is the writer a millionaire? Did he become a millionaire by marketing his "how to be a millionaire" books? Study about the writer or writers before you buy a book or audio plan. Study the reviews and see what other people have said.

- They didn't feel they got anything from the previous programs they tried. At least their minds were subjected to hours of positive mental discipline. It's actually very difficult to read a book or listen to an audio plan and not acquire at least one beneficial idea or even a life-changing concept. Search for that one idea and most of the time you will discover many.

Now here are just a few of the benefits of reading and listening to positive, motivating and educational content.

- Never again feel like you're wasting your time. How much time do you spend each week driving your car, sitting on public transportation, exercising, or whatever other action you are in, or can be in, listening to material of your choice? How much time do you spend waiting, in lines, for commitments or for other people? This can be one of the most useful times of your life.

- It is motivating. We already know the power of motivation. Read or listen to the words of other optimists that inspire you and give you the mental strength to do almost anything you set your mind to.

- It is educational. Training should not stop after high school or college.

- To develop as a person we should spend our lives fertilizing our brains with valuable information. Like many careers that require ongoing training through seminars and conferences, you should take the continuing education to your own

personal achievement. Your success in life depends on it.

- We all need proper mental training. From the time we were added to this earth to this day, our minds have been programmed with negativity and confined beliefs. Some of this comes from our upbringing, friends, colleagues, the news we read and the commercials we watch. By focusing on the positive material, we can virtually recondition our minds and replace the negative and restrictive beliefs we have about success with positive and empowering ones.

Here is a process for capturing the best of nonfiction self-help content.

1. Study to understand. Personal development plans are full of facts and tips that work best when kept in conscious memory. Study or listen to the book or tape more than once. Each time you do, your information retention increases. Don't absorb too much data at once. The average mind begins to drift and snake around somewhere for twenty to thirty minutes. When this happens, ask for a break.

2. Evaluate. You probably don't have to trust everything you read or hear. Evaluate what the writer has to say with a clear mind. Does it make sense to you? If you followed the belief, would it improve your life? If so, why not make an effort? Don't be discouraged by the writer even if you disagree with most of what is said. Take what you can from the plan and leave the rest.

3. Implement. It is said that knowledge without application is not power; you can only probably do it. Use and implement what you learn in your daily life. Only then will the information be of real value to you.

4. To recap. Go back to your books, tapes, notes and plans often and consider how many times you have used the data. When you encounter the benefits, you will produce a passion for learning that is more acute than ever before.

5. Contribution. Make these books, tapes, and plans readily available to those you care about. Most people won't spend just a couple of dollars to buy their own book or tape, but they might read or listen to it if it's there.

Chapter 7: Getting organized

Commit to a positive environment. If your environment is full of garbage and disorganized, spending time to get organized will go a long way in helping you focus. Who can be positive sitting in the middle of a mess? An organized environment is eloquent and inspiring, a great place to establish a positive attitude.

Get moving

So you need to get organized. Well, like all of us. But now that you've set the organizational

goal, how do you successfully carry it out? Here are some tips on how to do it.

1. Start with the right job

This is crucial. Separate your organizational effort into sensible and traceable tasks, prioritize and start with a job that you think will give you the maximum return for the sweat you put into organizing and completing it. Folders are powerful tools. This could be a smaller job, which you know will be completed quickly enough, giving you the much-needed motivation boost to move on to the next big projects you've been dreading.

Or instead, it could be a bigger job that you know has been crying out for your attention for some time, and taking it off your plate will take the biggest load off your mind.

Take a moment if you need to determine this.

That time is advantageous, compared to the probable hours you can spend on a certain task, only to leave it unfinished in the middle.

2. Don't get sidetracked by micro-tasks

This is probably the common reason why attempts are made to organize bombs for many individuals.

You start organizing something, like your photo albums, and then you start looking at those photos and slide into the memories.

Before you know it, it's been a few hours, and you might even have had fun, but... those albums haven't moved.

A different example would be trying to organize a bunch of papers, only to wander off when you get to those tax papers, and start calculating your tax refund.

Be methodical and operational about it; if it's essential, set a sensible time limit for finishing each job, and make adherence to it a priority.

Tell yourself that once you're organized, you'll relax and spend an hour flipping through those albums, perhaps having a

well-deserved drink.

3. Produce a temporary staging area

As you clean up your mess, you may sometimes come across items that you haven't made room for, and you're not sure where to put them. You have two options for dealing with them: You can spend a little time thinking about where they go, and you can place them there. You can group similar things together, and assign them a basic place, based on where you need them most.

Instead, if you feel that figuring out what to do with them is taking a little time, or distracting you from your overall organizational attempt, you can put them in a "temporary assembly area," like a

cardboard box, with a mental note (or sticky note) to return to once the rest is done.

One caution, though - if you start throwing away everything you have about this temporary place, it will soon become one more mess that you will eventually have to deal with. And that kills your purpose.

4. Don't multitask

Don't be fooled into trying to do everything right away. Although this might seem more effective, in the long run it is not, as the chances are that it can lead to jumping back and forth between tasks, and you may end up not finishing anything.

Instead, assign a task or part of a task to someone else, if that's feasible.

5. Don't be a perfectionist

Last but not least, don't be a perfectionist when trying to fit everything into exactly specified places. Be flexible. Recognize that not everything can be perfect, and as long as you know where your things are, and can get to your items without any effort, you will be organized, even if it seems like a mess to the next individual.

Now that we've got the clutter out of the way and know how to organize, make sure you stay organized, and take the daily actions to keep it that way.

Chapter 8: Stay Focused

Focus on the positive things in your daily life. Don't focus on the things you don't want or the mistakes that happen. If you change your thoughts to the situation at hand, then you leave no room for anxious thoughts to dominate your thinking.

Put It All Together

Having an impression of what you want to achieve at all times, this leads it to manifest within your life. Look at yourself there and try to feel how you would feel if you were already there. The only thing stopping you from being there is you and completely you, so allow yourself to be there in any way imaginable. We are all capable of achieving our goals; it is only a matter of time. By visualizing or acting as if you have already achieved your goals, you will discover a new approach to why you are working toward your objectives.

If you are like me and you are working completely alone to achieve the goals you have set for yourself, then I advise you to break that work into small pieces. It's better and easier to work as if you were doing a puzzle, rather than making a 20-foot wall painting. This will help you stay motivated and focused due to the fact that you are relentlessly achieving small pieces of the goals.

Don't listen to the detractors, if someone

thinks you're a little crazy, or don't have confidence in what you can accomplish, then forget about them.

These people are a little upset that they don't have the drive, like you, to aim for the stars. Don't blame them entirely either; it's just that society has a way of disciplining people to stay in their safe and welcoming comfort zones. If you let them get to you, your center will disperse, and we don't want that.

Stay out of your comfort zone; succeeding is about accepting the risks and doing what is usually not done in our society - taking the low road. If you persist in your comfort zone, you will feel at ease and that may lead to not achieving your goals: drifting into limbo while looking for something to happen is never beneficial. Avoid your comfort zone, if you are feeling a little uncomfortable it may mean you are climbing into new and unfamiliar terrain that you have never been in, and that is exactly where you want to be.

Review everything you've accomplished at the end of the week to overload yourself, and then look at what tasks await you for the next week. This exercise keeps you focused by giving you concrete facts about where you've been and where you're going next.

Always write down everything you've been doing and everything you want to do. Use a planner, a calendar, an excel, a word, or whatever you want to use to write it all down, and go over it once or twice a week - but just do it!

Among the things that have always helped me with my goals is discussing them. I'll discuss where I am, the problems I need to fix, the new goals I've brought on my list, or how much work I have left to do to achieve any of them. By talking about your goals with trusted friends and even family members, you are supported in your thoughts and, who knows, they may even help you see something you don't have. It's always good to let it out, don't keep it a secret - silence is not the way, you need to discuss it.

Occasionally it is useful to leave a project or a goal you are working on for a few days to come up with something. You may find that once you're back on it, you can get a new angle on it that you may not have had before. This is where your mind subconsciously solves problems that it couldn't before, due to the fact that you never gave yourself the time to absorb it. It is as if you have planted a seed, if you stare at it for many days it may seem that it is not growing, but if you go away for a few days and come back to it, you will observe new things about it. This will give you energy, attracting a new focus to achieve your goals.

Among the most crucial things to keep in mind is that when you are closest to quitting is when you are actually closest to achieving your goals. If you feel you urgently need to give up on your goals, don't do it. I've been in many situations where I can't seem to go on, but that's just a mental block, a conditioned thing that you have inside of you that tries to keep you from reaching your goals. We are all prone to this pressure and most of us accept it. Don't follow the masses, you are different, if you continue, you will probably succeed. Just keep at it, and soon you will taste the true fruits of your labor.

Most individuals keep work and life on separate sides of the spectrum, when in fact it is necessary to mix them in a proper balance. Work is not negative, and it always tries to maintain this mentality. It is one of the things that gives us value. By making your work a part of your daily life, your goals will be achieved at a smoother and better pace and you will maintain a healthy focus.

Although you must always remember to keep your balance, don't get swallowed up by either of us or, if you get burned, you won't be useful to anyone.

Never let yourself get burned, and if you do,

take a vacation or something. I am very ambitious in all my goals, but I also respect the "out" sessions || from time to time. If you feel nauseous just looking at something you're supposed to be working on, then quit for a while and work on something else or try to relax. If you make time to relax, then you will refresh yourself. Each of us has a certain amount of leeway for anything before we have to recharge again. Know and respect your tolerance limit. Keep it balanced and even if you have to do something - you put it aside. By presenting yourself as a time to recharge and relax, you are in turn replenishing your focus meter so that you can continue without harming your productivity.

Chapter 9: Using Time Wisely

Avoid spending time in activities that are not in accordance with what you want in life. The crucial thing is to work consistently towards the activities that will make your life what you want and this in turn will help you have a positive attitude.

Time is precious

There are 24 hours in a day. At first glance it seems like a lot, but in our daily practical experience we often feel that there is never enough time to do all the things we want to do. How can we apply our time in such a way that we can make the most of those 24 hours?

A successful businessman once said, "If you want to succeed in life you have to give up sleep, television, or both. There is a lot of strength in these words. To use time wisely the first thing we can do is be aware of where we are not using time wisely, in other words, where we feel we are wasting our time. Television has brought many good things, but it is also true that it can take up much of our precious time unnecessarily. We can apply the time we save by watching less television by doing something constructive in our own lives or by doing something good for humanity.

Needless to say, sleep is absolutely necessary

and essential.

But sometimes we tend to afford to sleep more than we really need to, particularly on the weekend. So if we really prefer to write that novel, master that difficult piece on the piano or work out that fabulous business plan, we might have to be more economical in our sleep behavior.

Eight hours of sleep is suggested for good health. However, through the practice of meditation we can reduce step by step the amount of sleep we need. Eight hours can be converted into seven hours, six hours or even five or four hours, depending on our individual capacity. Because meditation provides us with inner peace, it can replace an amount of outer sleep. It is said that a moment of true inner peace that can be experienced in deep meditation can replace several hours of sleep.

Another thing that can help us use time more effectively is to alter the activity from time to time. By altering the activity we give ourselves a break. For our mind everything becomes boring and tedious after a while, so if we venture into a new activity the mind gets a new exuberance and energy. That new joy and energy will also help us to work much more concentrated and effectively. Then, when we have enough of that task we can go back to the old task and again get new joy and enthusiasm. "Rest is the change of activity," say some spiritual teachers. If we know how to use this little phrase of wisdom in our daily life, we will take a big step towards fulfilling our ambitions.

Chapter 10: Getting the Right Attitude

If you're not happy with your life, then it's up to you to alter it.

By developing the right attitude you are able to achieve anything you set your mind to.

Look at it the right way Attitude is not everything when it comes to success, but attitude plays a role in almost every phase of your life. A bad attitude gets more people fired than any other factor, and a good attitude gets people jobs and helps them keep them more than any other factor.

Your attitude affects many individuals, from your family to the stranger you smile at on the street corner. Your attitude is especially important when you are faced with seemingly hopeless situations. Losing a job, a partner or a friend because of a bad attitude is unfortunate... particularly because a bad attitude can be manipulated

.

You can find at least 2 ways to see virtually everything. A pessimist looks for difficulty in opportunity, while an optimist looks for opportunity in difficulty. A poet of long ago put the difference between optimism and pessimism in this way: "Two men watched from the prison bars - one saw mud, the other saw stars."

Unfortunately, many individuals look only at the problem and not at the opportunity that lies within the problem. Many employees complain about the difficulty of their jobs, for example, they do not realize that if the job were easy, the employer would hire someone with less skill at a lower salary. A small coin can hide even the sun if you hold it close enough to your eye. So when you get too close to your problems to think about them objectively, try to consider how your vision can be blocked, take a step back and look at the situation from a new angle. Look up instead of down.

Pessimism clouds the water of opportunity. Whenever a new innovation seems promising to make life easier, someone always complains that it is going to take the work of individuals. When Eli Whitney invented the cotton gin, objectors said it would put thousands of individuals out of work. Instead, the invention made the production of clothes much cheaper, and millions of individuals were able to afford more clothes, creating endless jobs. When the computer was invented, people believed that individuals would lose their jobs. Some individuals have had to retrain to remain marketable, but almost everyone agrees that computers have created - not eliminated - jobs and improved our capabilities without limit.

Nothing can be done to alter the fact that a problem exists, but much can be done to find opportunity within that problem.

A better tomorrow is guaranteed by doing your best today and formulating a plan of action for the tomorrows ahead. Just

remember to maintain a positive mental attitude so that, when planning for tomorrow, you do so with a sense of anticipation that produces substantially better results.

The culprits still believe that someone pushed Humpty Dumpty, and would vote against starting a Pessimist Club since they don't believe such a club can work.

Almost half of the workers fall into the cynical class. They distrust almost everything - the government, big business, the products they buy, their employer, supervisors and co-workers.

An additional portion of workers are classified as cautious, with strong cynical leanings.

How many friends and how much peace do cynics have? How well do they get along with their spouses, children, and neighbors? Not many, not much, and not very well.

On the sunnier side of life are the idealists, people who have a tendency to see the best solution in any position. Sow those seeds of optimism, and you will raise the optimism within you.

Much cynicism is induced by unrealistic expectations - expecting great things to happen to you without any effort on your part. Having high expectations for yourself is a crucial part of success, but you must also develop a solid program of goals to realize those expectations. Individuals too often see the world through rose-colored glasses, and when their unrealistic expectations fall short, they become cynical and put on rose-colored glasses.

Have you ever been stuck in a traffic jam at the worst possible time?

Have you stepped on your foot, hit the wheel, shook your fist and leaned against the horn? If so, did you find that the louder you blew the horn and the more you needed it when you shook your fist, the faster the traffic would open up in front of you and let you pass?

If you follow that act of stepping on your foot and honking often enough, you will raise your blood pressure, increase your chances of having a heart attack or getting ulcers, and generally ruin your disposition and shorten your life.

Consider that jam, smile and say, "Wow, I bet it's going to take at least a half hour to get through this mess! In half an hour, if I listen to information tapes, I add to my vocabulary, I find new principles of leadership, or I increase my knowledge!" Or if you have someone in the car with you, a traffic jam is an opportunity for an uninterrupted visit. Use the time to complete a shopping list or plan a surprise for your classmates on the next birthday. Your choices may not be abundant, but using your time to do meaningful things is better than "stewing without doing.

You have a choice: you can either win or get something while you wait, or you can become distressed and cause strokes, heart attacks, and hypertension. People jams" at the office, home, neighborhood, school, playground, and baseball stadium can be addressed in similar ways. Even if you can't play a tape or read a book when others' schedules don't fit your own, you can relax and watch people or use the extra time to work on ideas. You'll be healthier and happier at the end of the day if you take that approach.

Conclusion

Keep your focus and you will be able to become a positive person. Now is the time to adopt these powerful techniques for success and you will live a happier, more rewarding life now and in the future.

Let's hope this book has given you the tools to start on the path to becoming more positive!

7 POWERFUL
SECRETS
POSITIVE
THINKING

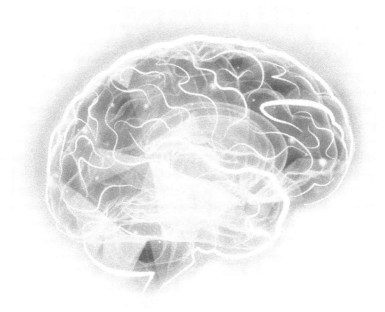

BOOK 2

7 POWERFUL SECRETS POSITIVE THINKING

Introduction

You've heard of positive thinking, you may have even read about it. Maybe you've begun to recognize that it's time to change who you are and become a more positive person.

Well, I'm glad you did.

Throughout this book, you will learn some deep concepts about positive thinking. You'll be taking in a lot of information... be prepared to learn and practice some valuable tools to help you banish the negative and welcome the positive.

Are you ready?

Great - let's get started!

First secret: The Mind/Body Connection

Did you know that thought is an action? Think about that for a moment... thinking is an action. The mind is the place where thought occurs!

I guess you rarely consider the act of thinking.

It's just something that happens while you're going about your daily life.

With our busy lives, not many of us take the

time to sit and think. Our hectic lives result in thinking that is more instinctive and rarely planned.

You may find this hard to believe, but before you said good morning to a family member, the thought of those words existed in your mind. Even before the words were spoken.

Besides, without thinking, we can't move our bodies.

For example, think about the process of raising your hand.

No, don't think about it - go ahead and raise your hand.

Do you know what is happening?

Well, it is a complicated process in which the muscle contracts causing the hand to move.

A nerve impulse causes the muscle to contract. An action in the brain sends the impulse along the nerve.

The brain, nerve and muscle work together like the parts of a machine our body would have. The machine that is our body would not have any action the power of the mind.

What about will power? Can we affect change in our life by using our will power?

You can try to get your hand up as much as you want. However, unless the mind thinks something completely different from the thought of the will - the hand remains still.

Have you ever gone on a diet? Willpower alone probably didn't help you lose weight; you had to change the way you thought about food and exercise.

Body action is the result of mental action.

What does all this have to do with positive thinking? Be patient... we're getting there.

From time to time, we are not in control of our mind.

The forces of the outside world make the mind act.

What happens if a child runs out in front of your car? A frightening thought. I'm sure you'd instinctively hit the brakes.

If your mind hadn't taken action, you would have run into the child.

There would be no bodily action... the hitting of the brakes... without the action of the mind.

Although many external events influence the mind, the mind is the power behind everything else to move the body.

Without the mind, there would be no
movement.

We can prove this profound statement by
thinking of the moment when there is no
mind, as in death. The body cannot move.
The nerves, muscles, tendons and bones are
parts of the machine that the mind uses.

By themselves, any part of the machine (our
body) is as helpless as a lever when a person
does not grab it.

Why stress the connection between mind and
body? Well, if thinking has such an impact
on what we do, then it is important to think
the right thoughts.

Think about your own life for a moment. Do you feel energized and ready to face the world when your mind is full of negativity?

Do you feel productive and satisfied?

I guess you answered NO.

The simple truth is... positive thoughts will give you better results than negative ones. Positive thinkers discover constructive results in all aspects of their lives...business, relationships, and personal satisfaction.

If you employ the power of positive thinking, you are likely to conjure up pleasant feelings and productive images.

More energy and happiness may emanate, which will have a positive impact on your daily life. You may exude more energy and happiness, which will have a positive impact on your daily life and constructive outcomes in all aspects of your life.

Remember, the combination of brain, nerves, muscles, ligaments, bones - these form a wonderful machine that the mind builds and uses. You need to make sure your mind is full of positive thoughts to benefit from the power of positive thinking.

Thinking the right thoughts, positive thoughts have powerful impacts on all areas of our lives (we will learn more about these impacts as we go along).

In Secret #2, we will learn about emotions and how they affect our well-being. Some things may surprise you...

Second secret: Emotions and their effect on well-being

In Secret #1, we learned that the mind and the body are strongly connected. Because of that connection, we learned that it is vitally important to think the right thoughts.

It turns out that those thoughts also affect our emotions. And, the vast array of emotions we experience daily has a profound impact on our well-being.

Our daily emotions can range from satisfaction to anger, from jealousy to rage, from joy to sadness. Each of these emotions has an impact. Every emotion affects the body.

I wonder if you have ever been in a situation where it was inappropriate to laugh (let's say during a serious presentation).

Did something overtake you and you found yourself bursting out laughing at the most inopportune moment?

Well, if that scenario had happened to you, you would have experienced unintended action. An unintended action is basically something your body does that you didn't want it to do.

A person doesn't usually shed tears because they choose to. Tears are not welcome and typically follow an effort to suppress them.

Why do tears flow?

Well, when the mind is filled with sadness or distress, an unintentional action causes increased activity in the tear glands.

The fluid is produced in excessive quantity and the eyes overflow. Even if you did not intend to cry, the thought that preceded the crying caused it to happen. A means to make it happen.

An example of an unintentional action.

When the sad thoughts subside, the tears no longer flow and the facial muscles return to normal.

What are some of the unintended actions of other emotions?

Have you noticed the physical changes your body goes through when you are angry?

- Does your heart beat faster?

- Does your blood pressure rise?

- Does your face blush or turn pale?

- What about when you are scared?

- Do you wake up in a cold sweat?

- Do you experience severe muscle tension?

- Do you clench your teeth?

All of the bodily reactions described are unintentional and occur when you are experiencing emotions such as fear or anger. Some of these reactions, such as increased blood pressure, may have a detrimental effect on your health.

Very different bodily changes occur if the thinking is of a humorous, witty or happy nature. The muscles of the chest, throat, and face react through laughter and smiling to show their pleasure. You feel the beneficial flow of more oxygen to your brain.

Your muscles and your breath move in response to the actions of your mind, even though it was not your intention to move them. And, the laughter and smile you experience will not stop until the thought that produced the reaction ceases. The laughter and smile can even be renewed by the renewal of that thought.

I am sure you have found yourself smiling at your desk when you remember an incident or a funny joke. Just the thought of that pleasant memory can make you smile again...

We have shown that the physiological changes your body undergoes when faced with different emotions are numerous.

When you think positively, your body also reacts positively.

Negative thoughts such as fear, sadness and anger cause physiological reactions that have a powerful negative impact on the body.

The mind-body connection can be so strong that some people when they hear bad news react by having serious digestion problems. Others may experience a debilitating headache.

With the obvious distress the body

experiences in reaction to negative thoughts or feelings, it becomes even more important to employ positive thinking techniques.

With positive thinking, your body experiences stress in a positive way, your body relieving reactions such as laughter and smiling instead.

React positively.

With negative thinking, your body experiences stress-inducing reactions such as increased blood pressure and adrenaline.

Positive thinking isn't all rosy. What I mean is that positive thinking does not mean going around pretending that everything in life is

perfect.

Positive thinkers are optimistic and realistic in the face of everyday adversity. They look for the positive in people, situations and experiences.

In contrast, negative thinkers focus on the bad and may even have stress-related health problems.

Negative thinkers may also find that people become less tolerant of their negativity and do everything possible to avoid being around them.

Want to know what you can do?

The next time you find yourself responding negatively to a situation or experience, think about the physiological impact the negative reaction is having on your body.

Think about the stress on your heart. Feel your blood pressure rise. Recognize that your negative response is having a detrimental effect on your body.

Perhaps by thinking about all the negative impacts that your discordant thinking is having on your body and your health - it will help you on your way to positive thinking.

What have we learned?

Thinking affects our emotions.

The physiology of our body changes when we experience different emotions.

Negative thinking...

Causes negative emotions.

Causes physiological changes with a negative impact on our body.

Positive thinking...

Causes positive emotions.

Causes physiological changes with a positive

impact on our body.

Are you confused about how to control your negative thoughts so that you can begin to see the positive impacts on your body? Then stay tuned for Secret #3 where we learn about how to control our thoughts...

Third secret: How to control your thinking

So far we have learned that there is an incredibly strong connection between our minds and our bodies. So strong, in fact, that our thinking impacts our emotions.

Our bodies have strong physiological responses to whatever emotions we're experiencing. Negative emotions such as fear and anger cause negative bodily actions such as increased blood pressure. Positive emotions like peace and happiness cause positive bodily responses like increased flow of oxygen to the brain!

What awaits Secret #3? Here you will learn how to control your thinking so you can have those positive physiological responses in your body... instead of the negative ones. Not to mention all the other wonderful benefits of positive thinking.

How do you apply the power of positive thinking in your own life?

The answer is simple...

STOP THINKING NEGATIVE THOUGHTS...

Easier said than done, right?

Of course I won't leave you hanging, we will learn about the importance of controlling your positive thoughts and emotions to eliminate those negative thoughts

One way to control your thinking is to stop the bloodshed. Change the flow of your negative thoughts to the brain and think about harmonious thoughts.

Surprisingly, parents or caregivers of children regularly apply this principle to stop negative thinking.

DISTRACTION

For example, when a child is upset because another child has taken a toy from him, the parent or caregiver will try to draw the child's attention away from the negative situation.

If the child sits there and stares at the other child who took the toy away from him or her... the crying will continue. However, if that child is distracted to start thinking about something else, for example, the cute puppy playing in the yard, he has gone from having negative thoughts about the lost toy to having positive thoughts about the cute puppy.

The requirement to 'drop your negative thoughts' - to let go like a stone in your hand - can be difficult. But I want to point out that dropping the negative thought requires much less effort in the long run than maintaining the negativity.

Controlling your thinking is one of the primary actions of your mind. Like all actions, it can be difficult to describe.

You can ask someone to 'give you a book' but it is impossible to instruct that person on how to move his or her hand.

There are three mental actions that are essential to the training of your thought control.

- How to think.

- How to stop thinking any particular thought that may be in your mind.

- How to change the thought from one thought to another.

While you are reading this book, you may be thinking, "It won't be that easy to stop thinking my negative thoughts.

Well, early scholars of positive thinking research disagreed.

Edward Carpenter stated profoundly in the early 20th century, "If a pebble in our boot torments us, we drive it out. We take off our boot and shake it off. And once the matter is fairly well understood, it is as easy to expel an intrusive and unpleasant thought from the mind as it is to shake a pebble from the shoe;

and until a man can do that, there is no point in talking about his ancestry over nature and everything else. He is a mere slave and prey to the bat-winged ghosts that fit in the corridors of his own brain.

When a negative thought slips into your mind, you have the power to choose to banish the negative thought and when a negative thought appears try to think of a more uplifting one. The thought creeps into your mind.

Try this mental exercise to help you STOP the negative thought. You have the power to banish them.

We all experience the frustrations of driving. In fact, driving is considered one of the most intense daily stressors we experience. If you find yourself reacting disapprovingly to a fellow driver, and feel those negative thoughts seeping in, try to change the image in your mind. Think of something that will calm you down or lift your spirits. Maybe it's your favorite vacation spot.

Maybe it's the smile on a young child's face. Whatever it is... shift your focus to that thought instead of the frustrating driver.

I hope that by doing this mental exercise, you will realize that you have let go of the fleeting frustration and have continued to drive with a much calmer and more peaceful outlook.

If you really want to experience the "POWER

OF POSITIVE THOUGHT", you need to practice seriously. You will need to persevere.

If you do everything you can to stop negative thinking, in the way that your own knowledge and experience suggest, you will learn the lessons of positive thinking.

You may learn more about yourself than you thought possible! The serious practitioner of positive thinking will gain an understanding and power that will enable him to do what seemed impossible at first.

In this Secret, we demonstrate a couple of tools to control our thinking.

We will continue the journey in Secret #4 where we show that our reactions to unplanned external events will be very different when we practice the power of positive thinking.

Fourth secret: How to react to external events in your life

Since we are in the middle of our journey, this is a good time to reflect on some of the secrets we have learned as we travel along the path of self-development.

Secret #1 - The mind and the body are so connected that we need to make sure we have positive thoughts to experience a positive impact on the body.

Secret #2 - Our body has strong physiological responses to the emotions we are experiencing. If we choose to think positively, we will experience positive emotions. If we experience positive emotions, our body receives the positive health benefits rather than the negative health impacts such as stress and high blood pressure.

Secret #3 - You can choose to banish negative thoughts!

When negative thoughts invade your mind, remember to use the visualization technique and take your mind to a quieter, more peaceful place.

Let's move on to Secret #4, where you will discover the 'right' way to react to external events in your life.

It is a fact of life that you will experience events in your life that were not planned or desired. How you react to these events says a great deal about the kind of person you are.

That is a concept that must be understood. An example will probably help you internalize this concept.

Perhaps you are camping in the woods and discover that a wild bear is running toward a small child at a neighboring campground. Several people witness the situation.

A person with a vivid imagination imagines all the horrors that can happen and is paralyzed by fear.

Another person thinks only of himself and his danger, and runs away to escape the danger.

Another faint instantly from fear. His fainting arises from his mental anxiety and only adds to the confusion of the situation.

One woman was so engrossed in setting up her tent that she did not see the wild bear, so she would not have been disturbed by it, nor would she have taken any action related to it.

Another, seeing the exact same situation of the bear attack, pending that others are experiencing, is triggered by a completely different line of thought. Remember that very

loud noises distract bears from their course of action.

So, bang on the lids of the pots and scream at the top of your lungs, making the bear stop paying attention to the child. With this reaction, another adult may snatch the child and run away to safety.

In the example described, we have an external incident of the bear's attack, each person's thought and subsequent bodily action. Each action in the illustration was connected to the same incident, however the resulting actions were from the person's thought and not from the actual incident of the bear's attack.

What is the relevance between our

illustration of the bear attack and positive thinking?

Well, the example shows that it is not the incident you are experiencing that causes your actions; it is the thought about the incidents that causes it.

Therefore, when you are faced with a negative situation in your life, such as the loss of your job, your resulting actions will depend on how you think about your circumstances.

If you think that losing your job means that you are worthless and cannot work, then your relationship actions will be negative. You may sit on the couch for days watching meaningless soap operas. Your actions are

having a negative impact on your life and are causing you to regress.

What if you choose to be positive? What would happen then? What would happen if you focused on the positive side of losing your job? Perhaps you think about that now that you have the opportunity to explore a new career that has always intrigued you, then your resulting actions will be completely different.

You can do research to improve your education. Think that you will have plenty of time to learn more about your desired field. Your actions are having a positive or negative situation..., your impact on our life is moving you forward, the resulting actions depend on how you think about your circumstances.

These examples illustrate that in each case, it is not the external incident, but your own thought that directs...controls...and decides what your course of action will be.

Therefore, it is obvious then that thinking about situations and experiences in a positive way will cause you to take a positive course of action.

Do you think you can begin to apply this concept in your own life?

Why not start today? The next time you are faced with an adverse experience, consciously choose to think positively. You may be surprised at how different you will act as a result.

I know it can be difficult to apply positive thinking every day. Think of this book as your motivation to keep going.

Consider Norman Vincent Peale's famous quote from the book, The Power of Positive Thinking. He states, "Motivation is like nutrition. It must be taken daily and in healthy doses to maintain it. "

That's it! In Secret #4 of our journey to positive thinking, we learned how important it is to react to unplanned adverse events in a positive way. Our positive thinking will keep us on track and ensure that our reaction to the event is positive.

I was wondering... would you like to be more productive in all aspects of your life? Stupid question... right? We all want to be more productive. Well, Secret #5 uncovers the truth behind the fact that positive thinkers are people who are more productive!

Fifth secret: Enjoy a productive life... with positive thoughts

I hope you've started to apply some of the ideas from our first four secrets. There's no reason to wait - the sooner you start, the sooner you'll see the results!

Among the wells of wisdom today is a small, "old" quote that never seems to show its age: "A journey of a thousand miles begins with a single step.

In our last Secret, you learned to 'react' to unplanned events in your life. Instead of seeing an unexpected event as a negative, you will have a feeling of accomplishment if you try to see the positive instead. For example, try to focus on the opportunity that underlies the unplanned event.

"Most successful men have not achieved their distinction because they have been presented with some new talent or opportunity. They have developed the opportunity that was within their grasp.~ Bruce Barton, American author

There are many interesting books that show that positive thinkers are some of the most successful leaders of our time. These leaders do not let obstacles such as unplanned external events stand in their way. They reach out to their surroundings with a positive attitude and rise up to success!

Prolonged grief, fear and anger can shorten your life.

Anxiety, doubt and despair can cripple our productivity.

Bitterness, greed, lust, jealousy and envy can cause successful people to commit illicit and criminal acts.

Conversely, contentment, peace and satisfaction can produce beneficial effects. In fact, they can prolong your life!

I have read many studies on positive and negative thoughts and their impact on the body and actions. Here is an interesting experiment, conducted in the early 1900s, that I thought I would share with you. This study was at the forefront of demonstrating the relationship between productivity and positive/negative thoughts.

Imagine who came up with this study! A study has shown that hair grows more slowly when a person is subjected to several months of anxiety!

Now, in the study...

A professor designed a regulated spring to maintain a uniform degree of resistance and to record the number of times it was pressed. The test subjects had to press the spring with their finger until, due to exhaustion, the finger refused to act. This part of the test determined the average number of times the spring was pressed, under normal circumstances, before exhaustion occurred.

Days later, the same subject was asked to think about some subject that caused dissonant thoughts, such as what was the saddest thing that had happened to him or to the person he hated the most. After a long period of time thinking about the subject, so that his mind would be filled with inharmonious thoughts, he was asked to press the spring.

Can you guess what happened?

You are right; the average number of depressions performed under the negative mental conditions was much less than that of

ordinary circumstances.

What happened when the subject thought about such things as love, peace, and happiness?

You guessed right again - the number of times the spring was pressed was much higher than the number performed under ordinary circumstances.

It is hard to believe that an experiment performed so long ago has the same relevance today.

Think about your own life for a second. Have you noticed that you have much less physical or mental exhaustion after a pleasant day at work than one that is occupied in unpleasant or stressful situations? I know I have. I'm always motivated to do more at night after a nice day at work.

Before I applied positive thinking techniques in my own life, I was more likely to want to sit on the couch after a stressful and exhausting day.

The professor who conducted the experiment we just outlined had a theory that the physical or mental exhaustion that follows a stressful day is caused by the absurd feelings of hurry, tension, and anxiety. In other words, uncertainty, anxiety, worry, and fear break a person down. But, if the mind is filled with thoughts of calm, security, courage, and confidence, then a person can be much more productive.

How can a decades-old experiment be applied to the vastly changed world of the 21st century?

Well, deep down, you have to make sure you keep a positive thought... no matter what you're putting up with in your workday.

I'd like you to try this mental exercise, the next time a co-worker or a client does something that would normally make you angry...

Instead of thinking about 'how you got it wrong', try thinking about something positive... like the next vacation or the lovely thing your child said to you the other day.

Highlight the negativity that is draining you and pass it on to your positive thoughts.

It is important to remember that having a positive attitude and using your positive thinking is essential! Positive thinking will help you stay focused, re-energize your body and improve your productivity!

In short, positive thinking influences your productivity.

Do you know how to look for the good in others and in experiences? If not, Secret #6 will help you learn how!

Sixth secret: Looking for the good

In Secret #5, we discovered that the application of positive thinking has the added benefit of making us more productive.

Plus, if you're like most people, you're living an accelerated life and would find that being more productive is very beneficial!

To help you continue on your path to positive thinking, it's time to learn to "look for the good" and that's what Secret #6 is all about.

Your mother may have told you to "always try to see the good in people. And as much as we hate to admit that our mothers are always right - in this case, she was right!

Seeking the good in others' is probably something you were taught to do in your early education. Elementary school teachers have the advantage of helping children learn to keep an open mind about others and experiences. Now, as an adult, you like the idea, but you may have trouble applying this principle in your daily life.

It turns out that looking for the good in people and experiences is a great way to turn your thoughts from the negative into positive, more harmonious thoughts. Remember, apply this idea to both people and experiences.

Consider that even the people you may consider as evil, Looking for the lazy or insignificant have some good qualities and have done some good deeds.

Also, consider that even experiences that you consider to be out of time from places you would rather not be, may have some good underlying qualities.

It is generally accepted that there was never a person who did not have some good qualities or did some good deeds. There has never been an experience that did not have some good in it, or that was not closely related to it.

The pursuit of good, if it is diligent and faithful, does not have to be in vain. When you find the good, remember to treasure what you have achieved. When your habit of seeking the good in others is fully established, negative thoughts will rarely intrude.

Let us illustrate the theory of finding the good in experiences with an example.

A young woman living on a busy street in Buenos Aires complained that she could not sleep because the noises of the busy city street outside her house disturbed her. A colleague of hers suggested that every noise, whatever it might be, had a musical note to it and she should try to find that note in each of the various sounds she heard.

She decided to give it a try. She gave up all attempts to fall asleep and set about looking for the musical note among the city street noises. Not surprisingly, he slept soundly all night.

Why could he find the deep sleep that had eluded him for so long? The explanation is that she had previously concentrated on the discordant characteristics of the noises she heard, and by thinking about these thoughts, she expanded her awareness of the negative, and remained awake.

In her search for the musical notes, she lost sight of the disturbing negative conditions, and she fell asleep because the discordance of the noises no longer disturbed her. She let her mind concentrate and got the desired result.

The search for the good in others and in

experiences, is one of the best methods to replace negative thinking with positive and consistent thinking. One piece of advice, don't limit your attempt to seek the good just "in the moment.

What I mean is that when you have a negative experience or with a negative person, don't go "oh yes, I have to look for the good in people and experiences".

Instead, consider looking for the good as a "life's work," constantly working to eliminate negative thoughts.

When you are able to change your thinking so that you always "look for the good," you will discover that your life will shine brighter and brighter.

Not just for you - but also for those around you... family, associates, co-workers, employees and friends. The obvious fact is that people are inclined and want to spend time with others who are looking for the good in people and experiences.

Perhaps you have someone in your life right now who exudes the lifestyle of positive thinking. Others are likely to comment on how positive they are; that no matter what happens, they always see the positive side. They may comment on your positive attitude and that it is nice to be around you and that not one negative word comes out of your mouth.

I hope you will reflect on this Secret the next

time you feel a negative thought about a particular person or experience. If you stop and reflect on what is good about that person or experience, I promise you will put that negative thought aside.

That ends Secret #6! In the final Secret, we will take a moment to reflect on learning our first six Secrets and discuss how this transformation to positive thinking 'isn't always easy'.

Recognizing that you will have some challenges on your journey can help you stay on course to become a positive thinker. However, nothing that is good in life is easy... is it?

I thought this quote from Sir James M. Barrie

was appropriate for today's topic.

"The secret of happiness is not in doing what
you like, but in liking what you do. "

Seventh secret: It's not always easy

Here we are, at the end of our journey. Time has flown by... I trust you have been able to take some of the ideas we have learned so far and apply them to your own life.

Let us take the time to reflect on what we have learned during our six previous stops.

We started again at Secret #1 and learned that the mind and the body are so interconnected, that to ensure a healthy body, we must think the right thoughts... positive thoughts.

That led us to Secret #2, which explained that our bodies have very strong physiological responses to our emotions. In fact, if we have positive thoughts, we will benefit from the body's positive reactions. Of course, the opposite is also true.

Secret #3 showed you that you could choose to banish your negative thoughts! You can learn to control your thinking - it takes perseverance and practice.

Our next Secret, #4, demonstrated how important it is to have a positive reaction to unplanned external events. We discovered that a positive response would put you on a positive track.

In Secret #5, you learned how positive thinking can actually make you more productive. I'm sure you will reap great benefits in both your personal and professional life by being more productive.

Secret #6 focused on looking for the good in others and in experiences. Practicing this theory can help you banish negative thoughts from your life-forever.

Without further ado, let's start with Secret #7 where we'll talk about how this journey to becoming a positive thinker won't always be easy.

Have you ever noticed that the best achievements in your life were not always easy?

Maybe you had to work long hours to get that promotion that catapulted you into your dream job.

Maybe you spent the first year of your child's life existing with very little sleep. Maybe you even sacrificed an exciting youth to get stellar grades in college or university.

I bet when you look back on your accomplishments, your memories of the difficulties of getting there have long since faded.

The same goes for the acquisition of the power of positive thinking.

IT'S NOT ALWAYS EASY...

An established habit of any kind is not broken by a few weak ones.

Persistence and determined effort will overcome even the most dominant habit. I know that you can overcome the dreaded ingrained habit of allowing the negative to permeate your mind!

It is hard to believe, but Aristotle was in control of habits in his time.

"We are what we repeatedly do. Excellence, then, is not an art, but a habit.

The necessary condition for success in changing your mental thoughts from the negative to the positive is **PERSISTENCE**.

Every time the negative thoughts you are trying to banish reappear - you must have the ability to persist.

Persistence really shouldn't be too difficult to achieve.

The beauty of the power of positive thinking is that you can practice it anywhere, under any circumstances and in connection with whatever your career or personal situation.

You must be your own instructor because others cannot instruct you. Instructors do not

own your thoughts.

You must select and earn your own lessons and discover and correct your own mistakes.

I recognize how difficult this journey can be. I guarantee that perseverance, persistence and determination to succeed will overcome any obstacles and lead you to success.

Perhaps you have already succeeded on some occasions in banishing your negative thinking. The real question is...

Have you banished negative thinking forever?

Your answer is probably no, but don't despair.

The fact is that you have had some previous success, even in a limited way, which shows that you have the ability to practice positive thinking.

What a person has accomplished once, they can accomplish again.

This point is important because it indicates that complete success in banishing negative thoughts is attainable, despite the difficulties you may encounter.

Perseverance in changing your habits of negative thinking to habits of positive thinking is essential.

Orison Swett Marden made this profound statement about habits that I think is very appropriate when thinking about learning positive thinking...

"The beginning of a habit is in an invisible thread, but each time we repeat the act we strengthen the thread, and add another strand, until it becomes a great wire and binds us irrevocably, thought and act. "

Don't be discouraged. Remember that major or minor events will come into your life from time to time - that's understandable.

You may even have incidents that look like failures, but they can all be overcome and turned into successes.

Remember that every time you recognize the pervasiveness of your negative thoughts, you are learning.

Perseverance is essential.

There is an old Chinese proverb that says, "Be careful to the end as in the beginning, and you will not fail in your enterprise.

To achieve greatness, to gain the power of positive thinking, you must persevere. It is the only possible course of action if you really want to succeed in changing your life through positive thinking.

I truly believe in the power of positive thinking and the profound changes it can make in your life. I hope you are beginning to see the great impact positive thinking can have on your life.

Your journey can be difficult at times. Always remember that your greatest achievements often come after hard work and perseverance.

I have enjoyed our journey together and I really hope you can capture all the wonder and power of positive thinking.

I wish you all the best!